VIKING

GOOGLE ADVERTISING

Viking Google Advertising Page

Chapter 1:

Intro to Google Advertising

Google is without question the world's premiere search engine. But it's become even more than a search engine since it's humble beginnings. Today, it also happens to have what is arguably the most powerful and far-reaching advertising network in the world.

Today, with Google AdWords, you can put your offers in front of motivated buyers as sponsored search results. This means people are seeing your ad at the very moment they are searching for your solution. What could be more powerful than that?

Then there's the Display Network. Ever notice all those image ads in the side bars, top, and bottom of almost every website you visit? And more banners mixed in within content? Often retargeting ads for a product you recently viewed? There's a good chance most of those were part of the Google Display Network.

When you combine the perfect timing of search result ads and the far-reach of the display network with the very reasonable cost per click of Google AdWords... it becomes a must-have advertising solution.

Here's some stats that paint a clear picture of why you should be using Google Ads. Google owns over 70% of the search market share. They officially have the world's largest ad network. Google's display campaigns reach a whopping 80% of global internet users. When people see display ads, they are over 150% more likely to search for brand and segment-specific keywords.

And even if you were planning to just focus on organic SEO, you need to have Google ads in the mix. Almost 90% of traffic from search ads is NOT replaced by organic clicks when ads get paused. For people searching with real buyer intent, the ad spots at the top end up getting around 40% of the clicks on the SERPs. And almost 100% of searchers go with businesses they see on the first page of the SERPs, so getting those sponsored results up there is a must.

In case there was any doubt about the effectiveness of these ads, here's a few more stats. On average, marketers make $2 in sales for every $1 they spend on Google ads. On mobile, around 70% of searchers take action within one hour and 70% say they call businesses directly from Google Search (yes, you can have your clickable phone number right there in the ad). All these stats probably explain why over 70% of these businesses plan to increase their ad spend in the future.

So we've gone over why you should be using Google advertising in your business. Now let's talk about setting some goals.

Chapter 2:
Google Advertising Goals

Establishing advertising goals is critical to the success of your ad campaigns. Countless entrepreneurs and businesses have setup an advertising account, run a few ads, and then let it sit untouched for months or even years. This is usually due to a lack or absence of goals. So, before you even begin establishing any sort of advertising campaign or strategy, you need to establish clear advertising goals.

Your goals should be specific, measurable, and attainable. They can be long term, short term, or a mix of both. Deadlines and milestones can be helpful as well. "I want to increase my traffic and sales" would be an example of a bad goal that will likely result in your efforts petering out after a while because there are no specific milestones. "I want to generate 1,000 leads by Christmas" is an example of a good goal. It's specific, measurable, and certainly attainable. Below are some examples of the various goal categories you might be interested in.

Traffic to Website (Sales, Leads, Content)

Probably one of the most popular goals of advertising is to funnel traffic to your own web properties. You're leveraging paid advertising to obtain traffic and convert that traffic into brand-followers, leads, prospects, and customers. So maybe your goal is to get people to a landing page with a free offer where they can subscribe to your list and become a lead. Maybe they're being sent to a sales page or an ecommerce store. Maybe you just want to do some content marketing and send them to your blog. Whatever the case, the end goal for a lot of businesses will likely be bringing traffic over to their main web properties.

Social Following

In this goal category, your aim is to build a large number of followers. This usually means "likes or followers" in the case of a business/brand page or it could mean "friends" if you're focusing on your personal profile. The main sought-after benefit here is to increase the number of people who will see your posts or tweets in their feeds. In this sense, your social posts become similar to sending out email broadcasts via your autoresponder. It should be noted that some social networks have recently adjusted their algorithms in such a way that people tend to see less posts from businesses they've followed. This means a much smaller percentage of your followers will see your posts in their feeds today than did in the past. Still, if you grow a large enough community, this can still be very beneficial and if your content is engaging enough to get a lot of traction in the form of likes, comments, and shares, you can significantly increase the range of your organic reach into people's feeds. Paid advertising, either directly to your social platforms or to a page that encourages social following, can be a great way to accomplish this.

Brand Awareness

Another goal that's less thought about might be spreading brand awareness and recognition. If you're just starting out, there's a good chance your brand might be in need of a jumpstart. If nobody's ever heard of you, a great way to increase recognition is to simply flood the web with ads that direct people towards unique, helpful, or entertaining content and get your name, logo, and overall brand identity in front of as many people as possible as many times as possible. If this is your goal, you want to avoid being salesy in the beginning. Ensure you're focused almost entirely on funneling paid traffic to helpful, relevant, or entertaining content on your blog or other content channels.

Expand Existing Audiences

If you've already got an audience, your goal might be to make it bigger. Paid advertising can be used to direct traffic to viral content like a funny video that people will share. Other ways to expand existing audiences can include driving paid ads to contests, sweepstakes, and gamification systems. Assuming your offers/prizes are compelling enough, incentivized sharing and engagement can be very effective.

Enhancing or Repairing Public Relations

Do you want to set your company apart in the public eye? Do you want to associate your brand with feelings of good will and community involvement? If any of these apply to you, then enhancing or repairing public relations could certainly be a good advertising goal for your business.

Often, we hear about PR operations as being focused on damage control or repairing harm to a company's reputation, but it doesn't take a PR catastrophe to make PR enhancement a good idea. This is a goal that any business can engage in. Non-sales related campaigns can include photos or videos that foster positive values and goodwill or even involvement in social movements (be careful not alienate half your prospects) and noble causes. Did your business recently donate to a charity, build a school in a third world country, serve food at a local pantry? These are all things to send traffic to with ads. These don't necessarily need to be about things that your business participated in. They can be content about general things like a heart-warming video about helping the poor or caring for the elderly. Special holidays like Christmas, Thanksgiving, or Mother's Day also present opportunities to leverage emotions, foster goodwill, and enhance your PR.

Market Research

A hugely beneficial goal of paid advertising is market research. If you're just starting your business or going down a new path, you need to learn more about your audience and your market. Paid ads can get people to vote in polls, take surveys, or even drive them to the comment section of a blog where they'll share their opinions. Ultimately, your goal should be to gather as much data as possible and come up with one or two ideal customer avatars that you can then base your marketing and product development on.

All of the goals you've learned about in this section require some sort of overall strategy relying on the various types of advertising options. So that's what we'll be covering next.

Chapter 3:
Types of Advertising

Now that you've got your goals established, it's time to start cranking out some quality ads. Let's look at some of the types of ads you can create and leverage in your marketing.

Search Ads

Search ads are the ultimate "perfect timing" advertising method. These are ads that appear above, below, or next to search results. They are "native" which means they look more or less like organic search results, save for the single word "Ad" in a tiny box next to the url. These ads show up based on keywords that you targeted during the ad creation process, as well as any other criteria or parameters you specified such as geographic location.

The great thing about search ads is that you're literally putting your solution right in front of people exactly **where** they're looking and exactly <u>when</u> they're looking for it. The value of offering a product or service at the very moment someone is searching for it is absolutely priceless. What's more, you only pay when people click your ad or take another specified action like calling your business (yes, you can set up phone call ads). So even when people don't click, you're getting free exposure with your business name and brand being put in front of countless eyeballs.

Search Remarketing

As if search ads weren't already cool enough, with search remarketing you can take your ad spend efficiency and ROI to a whole new level. Unlike standard remarketing or retargeting which follows people around the web, search remarketing is still something that happens on the Search Engine Results Pages (SERPs). It allows you to show search ads specifically not just to people using your targeted keywords, but people using your targeted keyword **and** who were recently on one of your web properties. What does this mean? It means you are finetuning your ad campaigns, and your ad spending, down to a super-qualified group of prospects. This means more bang for your buck and greater ROI in the long term!

Display Ads

Google's display ads appear on more than 2 million websites around the web. If your audience is online, there's a very good chance they're spending time on a site that is part of the display ad network. And it's not just sites. These ads are displayed now on hundreds of thousands of mobile apps!

There are a few types of display ads. First, there's text. These are basic textual ads with a headline, a couple lines of text, and a url. Second, there's banner ads. These are the actual image ads that you see in the sidebars, the tops and bottoms of pages, and snuck in here and there in the middle of content as you scroll down through a blog or forum page. And it's not just plain images. These can be rich media, interactive elements, animated images and more! More recently you can even put your ads right inside of Gmail!

Video Ads

Arguably one of the coolest advertising developments in recent years, YouTube video ads are an incredibly powerful tool. All you need is a short video. This can be a talking head video of you, an animated video, anything. Using the AdWords ad creation process, you can then make YouTube ad that displays in front of relevant or targeted people on YouTube. Your video will appear either in the search results, in the related videos column, or can even play automatically at the beginning of other videos using the "TruView" system. Not only do you get to target and put these video ads in front of the perfect audience, but you only pay when people express interest in your ad!

So, all of these advertising methods are clearly great and present an incredible opportunity to help you grow your brand and your business. But none of this information is worth anything if you don't implement what you've learned. With that in mind, make sure you implement the steps of the following battle plan right away!

Battle Plan

Step 1: Determine your advertising goals.

Step 2: Get your relevant web properties ready to receive traffic.

Step 3: Do some research to determine best keywords and other parameters.

Step 4: Choose your best ad type and start creating ads!

www.ingramcontent.com/pod-product-compliance
Lightning Source LLC
Chambersburg PA
CBRC090851210326
41597CB00011B/172